# Climb Aboard the Poetry Plane

# Climb Aboard the Poetry Plane

Original Poems by John Foster

OXFORD
UNIVERSITY PRESS

# OXFORD
UNIVERSITY PRESS

Great Clarendon Street, Oxford OX2 6DP
Oxford University Press is a department of the University of Oxford.
It furthers the University's objective of excellence in research,
scholarship, and education by publishing worldwide in
Oxford New York Athens Auckland Bangkok Bogotá Buenos Aires
Calcutta Cape Town Chennai Dar es Salaam Delhi Florence Hong Kong
Istanbul Karachi Kuala Lumpur Madrid Melbourne Mexico City Mumbai
Nairobi Paris São Paulo Singapore Taipei Tokyo Toronto Warsaw

with associated companies in Berlin Ibadan

Oxford is a registered trade mark of Oxford University Press
in the UK and in certain other countries

Copyright © John Foster 2000
The moral rights of the author have been asserted
First published 2000

ISBN 0 19 276245 1

Typeset by StoreyBooks
Printed in Hong Kong

# Contents

The Poetry Plane        7
The Mermaid and the Fisherman        8
'I'm Bored,' Said Young Dragon        9
The Dragons' Flying Lesson        10
Our Teacher        11
The Spelling Bee        12
The Rules That Rule the School        13
Warnings        14
Inside Sir's Matchbox        15
Why do Teachers Call Me Emma?        16
Teacher        16
Size-Wise        17
Ten Things You Should Know About
     Hippopotamuses        18
Faxes From Dee        19
Counting Them Out        20
The Name of the Game        21
Word Whirls        22
Child Skipping        23
Ball Bouncing        24
Factory        25
Hotel        26
Belt        27
Shaun Short's Short Shorts        28
Nicola Nicholas        28
Boris Morris's Sister Doris        28
At the Animals' Fancy Dress Party        29
Castanets        29
If You Whistle at a Thistle        30
Riddle Me Hot, Riddle Me Cold        31
Colour Blind        32
Grounds for Recollection        32
The Price of Fame        33
The Price        34
News Flash        35

Show Me Your Scar, Please, Grandad     36
How Old Are You, Grandad?     37
Borrowed Time     38
There's a New Wooden Seat     39
I Stood All Alone in the Playground     40
My Little Sister     40
How Strange     41
My Baby Brother's Secrets     42
Moods     42
In My Dream     43
Museum Pieces     44
The Space Race     46
Space Thought     46
I Saw It on the News, Daddy     47
In a Fit of Rage     47
All That I Need     48
Black Crosses     48
The African Farmer's Song     49
Giraffe     50
Cats     51
The Guard Dog     52
Insects     53
The Bedbug's Story     54
Bird Talk     55
There's a Spring in Your Step     56
Spring Snow     56
Spring Sunshine     57
Summer     57
Gathering Storm     58
What Is Fog?     58
Heatwave     59
Cold Snap     60
Last Night It Froze     61
It's Diwali Tonight!     62
On New Year's Eve     62
I Spun a Star     63
December Day     64

## *The Poetry Plane*

Climb aboard the poetry plane,
And speed across the sky.
Visit worlds of wonder.
Let your imagination fly.

Circle castles in the clouds.
Watch mermaids flick their tails.
Hear the mighty dragons roar
And shake their shimmering scales.

Feel the flickerings of hope.
Taste anger's bitter tear.
Creep inside the monster's heart
And share his shivering fear.

Smell the scent of the wild rose.
Snorkle in coral seas.
Dance on the deck of a rainbow.
Float on the fluttering breeze.

Climb aboard the poetry plane,
And speed across the sky.
Visit worlds of wonder.
Let your imagination fly.

# The Mermaid and the Fisherman

By a cave of coral the mermaid sits
Beneath a silvery moon
And the lonely fisherman hears her voice
As she sings a haunting tune.

He forgets his nets and he grabs the oars
And he swings the boat around
To head for the shore for he must hear more
Of the soft bewitching sound.

By a cave of coral the mermaid smiles
Hearing the splash of an oar
And the grating of pebbles on the beach
As a boat is pulled ashore.

The fisherman stands in front of the cave
With a wild look in his eyes.
On a seaweed bed in a coral cave
An enchanting mermaid lies.

The fisherman reaches out with his hand
To touch her silvery hair
And the mermaid smiles as she lures him down
To capture him in her lair.

In a coral cave a fisherman sits,
Spellbound at a mermaid's side.
On the beach above an abandoned boat
Is lapped by the morning tide.

## 'I'm Bored,' Said Young Dragon

'I'm bored,' said young dragon,
'There's nothing to do.
The knights have all run away.
There's nothing to watch on the telly
And no one will come out to play.'

'Why don't you practise your roaring
Or revise for the fire-breathing test?
Or lie on your ledge at the back of the cave,
Read your book and have a good rest?'

'I'm not doing that! That's boring!'
Said young dragon, scratching the floor.
'Stop doing that!' roared his mother.
'You'll get dirt all over your claw.'

'I'm bored,' said young dragon,
'There's nothing to do.'
And he started to pick at a scale.
'Stop doing that!' roared his mother
And she gave him a flick with her tail.

'I'm bored,' said young dragon,
'There are no knights to fight.
Why can't I go out for a fly?
I'll watch out for planes and I promise
I won't fly too high in the sky.'

'Oh, all right,' said his mother, patting his wings,
'But listen carefully to me.
Don't you go near that castle
And be back here in time for your tea.'

## *The Dragons' Flying Lesson*

'Right,' said the flying instructor,
'Listen carefully to me.
Always make sure before you take off
You're not standing too close to a tree.

'Check for overhead power lines
And look out for telegraph wires.
Look right. Look left. Look up,
Before you ignite your fires.

'Once in the air, keep fully aware
By constantly swivelling your head,
And steer clear of airports and runways.
They are marked on your maps in red.

'Right, get your wings extended.
Inhale and prepare to blow.
Put your claws on your starters.
Count to three. Ready, steady, GO!'

## *Our Teacher*

Our teacher's a caterpillar.
During the day she crawls
Between the leaves of our desks
Picking holes in our writing
And chewing over our attempts
To wrestle meaning from our number-work.
At home-time she scuttles to the staffroom
And pulls on her overcoat
Like a chrysalis.
Later, in the quiet of her bedroom,
She transforms herself
Into a butterfly
Which dances the night away.
On the stroke of midnight,
She turns back into a caterpillar,
Crawls home to bed and sleeps,
Until the alarm-bell rings,
Summoning her to another morning's school.

## The Spelling Bee

Our teacher's got a Spelling Bee
Of which we're very wary.
It sits by itself on our teacher's shelf
Beside her dictionary.

Our teacher's got a Spelling Bee.
It buzzes round your head
Whenever you make a spelling mistake
And circles the word in red.

Our teacher's got a Spelling Bee
We treat it with respect.
It brushes your neck as it makes a check
That your spelling is correct.

Our teacher's got a Spelling Bee.
It keeps us on our toes.
Whenever we make a spelling mistake,
The Spelling Bee always knows.

Our teacher's got a Spelling Bee
Of which we're very wary.
It sits by itself on our teacher's shelf
Beside her dictionary.

## *The Rules That Rule the School*

Only speak when you're spoken to.
Don't stand and grin like a fool.
Pay attention or risk a detention.
We're the rules that rule the school.

Hands must not be in pockets
When addressing a member of staff.
Though smiling is sometimes permitted,
You need written permission to laugh.

Boys must stand to attention
And salute when they pass the Head.
Girls are expected to curtsy
And lower their eyes instead.

Sit up straight. Do as you're told,
If you want to come top of the class.
Bribes must be paid in cash
If you want to be sure to pass.

Don't breathe too loud in lessons.
Don't sweat too much in games.
Remember that teachers are human.
Don't *ever* call them names.

Only speak when you're spoken to.
Don't stand and grin like a fool.
Pay attention or risk a detention.
We're the rules that rule the school.

## *Warnings*

Do as you are told
In lessons on electricity,
Otherwise you could have
A shocking experience.

Keep your feet on the ground
In lessons on flight.
Remember Icarus.
Don't jump to conclusions.

## Inside Sir's Matchbox

Our teacher's pet
Lives in a nest of pencil-shavings
Inside a matchbox
Which he keeps
In the top drawer of his desk.
It's so tiny, he says,
You need a microscope to see it.
When we asked him what it ate,
He grinned and said,
'Nail clippings and strands of human hair —
Especially children's.'
Once on Open Day,
He put it out on the display table,
But we weren't allowed to open the box
Because it's allergic to light.

Our teacher says his pet's unique.
'Isn't it lonely?' we asked.
'Not with you lot around,' he said.

Once, there was an awful commotion
When it escaped
While he was opening the box
To check if it was all right.
But he managed to catch it
Before it got off his desk.

Since then, he hasn't taken it out much.
He says he thinks it's hibernating at present —
Or it could be pregnant.
If it is, he says,
There'll be enough babies
For us all to have one.

## Why do Teachers Call Me Emma?

Why do teachers call me Emma?
Emma isn't my name.
Though Emma and I are both tall and dark.
We don't really look the same.

Why do teachers call me Emma?
Why doesn't it occur
I'm not giggly and silly like Emma?
I'm not at all like her.

Why do teachers call me Emma?
Surely they can see
Outside I'm a bit like Emma,
But inside I'm Susan. I'm ME!


## Teacher

Tells us off.
Expects us to know the answers.
Always asking questions.
Crosses out our mistakes.
Hands out detentions.
Explodes if we chew gum.
Rapidly ageing.

## Size-Wise

Our teacher Mr Little's really tall.
He's twice the size of our helper Mrs Small.
'Were you big when you were little?'
Sandra asked him.
'I was Little when I was little,
but I've always been big!'
he said with a grin.
'Have you always been small?'
Sandra asked Mrs Small.
'No,' said Mrs Small.
'I was Short before I got married,
then I became Small.
But,' she added, 'I've always been little.'
'That's the long and the short of it,'
said Mr Little.
'I've always been big and Little,
but she used to be little and Short,
and now she's little and Small.'

## Ten Things You Should Know About Hippopotamuses

1.  What is a young female hippopotamus called?
    A hippopotamiss.

2.  What do parents say to a young hippo when telling him not to do something?
    A hippopotamustn't.

3.  How do you train a baby hippopotamus?
    By sitting him on a hippopotty.

4.  What does a hippo like spread on his burgers?
    Lots of hippopotamustard.

5.  What kind of dance music does a hippopotamus like?
    Hip-hop.

6.  What do you call a hippopotamus who says things behind other hippopotamuses' backs?
    A hippo-crit.

7.  What do you call a hippopotamus with chicken pox?
    A hippospotamus.

8.  What do you call a hippopotamus with a limp?
    A hoppopotamus.

9.  What do hippopotamuses shout when they're cheering somebody?
    Hip! Hip! Hooray!

10. What do you call a hippopotamus with a smile on its face?
    A happypotamus.

## Faxes From Dee

Sorry. Got held up. Will be an hour late.
        D. Lay

There are two sides to everything. We must talk.
        D. Bate

You're driving me out of my mind.
        D. Mented

I'll be down in a minute.
        D. Scend

I feel like giving up.
        D. Spair

In no way was I responsible.
        D. Ny

You can count on me.
        D. Pendable

That's it. My mind's made up.
        D. Cide

I can make your mouth water.
        D. Licious

## Counting Them Out

One's a singular sort of chap.
One stands alone. One knows one's place.
Two's a hypocrite with more than one face.
Three's a hat-trick punching the air.
Four's solid and strong. Four stands square.
Five is moody: a handshake or a fist.
Six's knickers are in a twist.
Is she six of one or half a dozen of the other?
Seven is wicked — the deadly sins.
Eight's a miser who grins with pleasure,
As he gloatingly counts his pieces of treasure.
Nine is a person who's had one too many.
Ten's a common lot you can get for a penny.

## The Name of the Game

Play with names
And Pat becomes tap.
Karl is a lark
And Pam is a map.

Miles is slime.
Liam is mail.
Bart is a brat.
Lina's a nail.

*Karl Lark*

*Liam Mail Tabitha Habitat*

*Norma Roman*

Stan tans.
Gary turns gray.
Norma's a Roman.
Amy makes May.

*Trish Shirt*

Tabitha's habitat.
Leon is lone.
Kate is teak.
Mona's a moan.

Trish is a shirt.
Kay is a yak.
But whatever you do,
Jack remains Jack.

# *Word Whirls*

On the wheel of words, words whirl, words twist, words swirl, words twirl.

Inside the wheel of words, words dance, words spin, words prance, words grin.

Words curl, words whirl.

# Child Skipping

```
        ki
    s       p
        ki
    s       p
        ki
    s       p
        ki
    s       p
        ki
    s       p
        ki
    s       p
        ki
    s       p
        ki
    s       p
        ki
```

# Ball Bouncing

B A L L A A A B A A A L L L L L L L L L L L A B A L L B A L L L W A L

*Factory*

*Hotel*

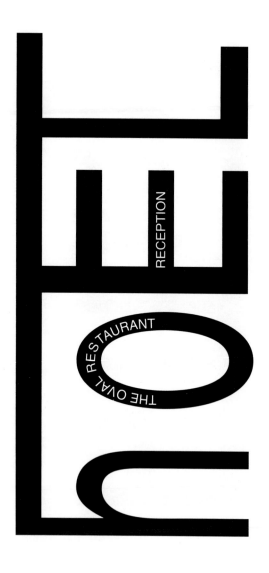

## *Belt*

I am a belt. Thread me carefully around your waist and fasten me tight or I might let you down.

belt

## Shaun Short's Short Shorts

Shaun Short bought some shorts.
The shorts were shorter than Shaun Short thought.
Shaun Short's short shorts were so short,
Shaun Short thought, Shaun, you ought
Not to have bought shorts so short.

## Nicola Nicholas

Nicola Nicholas couldn't care less.
Nicola Nicholas tore her dress.
Nicola Nicholas tore her knickers.
Now Nicola Nicholas is knickerless.

## Boris Morris's Sister Doris

Boris Morris had a sister Doris.
Horace Norris had a brother Maurice.
Boris Morris's sister Doris
Married Horace Norris's brother Maurice.
So Doris Morris became Doris Morris-Norris.

## At the Animals' Fancy Dress Party

At the animals' fancy dress party
The prize for looking most cute
Was won by the Emperor Penguin
Dressed in his birthday suit!

## Castanets

Castanets make mischievous pets,
For if given half a chance,
They click and clack, and snap and clap,
And lead you a merry dance.

## *If You Whistle at a Thistle*

If you whistle at a thistle
It'll turn its head.
If you compliment a carrot
It'll blush bright red.

If you squeeze a pickled onion
It'll start to cry.
If you cuddle a fresh cabbage
It'll softly sigh.

If you tickle a dill pickle
It'll give a girlish giggle.
If you stroke an artichoke
It'll squirm and wriggle.

If you caress a bunch of cress
It'll go quite weak.
But if you try to kiss a turnip
It'll slap you on the cheek!

## Riddle Me Hot, Riddle Me Cold

My first is in fish, but not in bone.
My second in iron, but not in stone.
My third in crown and also in throne.
My fourth once in twice,
But twice in returned.
Touch me, get burned!

My first is in wish, but not in bone.
My second is in rock, but not in stone.
My third once in twice,
But twice in tease.
Touch me and freeze!

Solution: 1. Fire 2. Ice

## Colour Blind

Football referees
Are peculiar fellows.
They think a red card
Is made out of two yellows.


## Grounds for Recollection

(An old footballer remembers)

'Do you remember *Anfield?*' he asked.
*Old Trafford* nodded his head.
'She lived down near the *Maine Road*
By *St Andrew's* church,' he said.

'*Molineux* her too,' he said,
'They went to *St James's* school.
They once pretended to find a *Goldstone*.
They were always playing the fool.

'They tore down *The Shed* and built *The New Den*
In *The Dell* by *The Riverside*.
They used sticks they took from *The Hawthorns*
And *Turf* from the *Moor* inside.

'Once for a lark, in *Goodison Park*,
They made all of us boys go trembly
By claiming they'd found on the C*ity's Ground*
A Cup Final ticket for *Wembley*!'

## *The Price of Fame*

It's not easy being famous.

Last week I was a hero.
In injury-time
my namesake scored the winner
with a glancing header.

Everyone ran round the playground,
chanting my name.

Today, I'm a villain.
Last night I missed an open goal.
Then, just after half-time,
I was sent off for a professional foul.
We lost two–nil.

Everyone's blaming me and calling me names.

If it goes on like this,
I'm going to ask Sir for a transfer.

## *The Price*

(During the 1980s, as part of State Plan 14.25, outstanding young athletes in the German Democratic Republic were regularly given drugs in order to boost their performances.)

'Oh yes, I won,' she said,
'I had my glory days.
Oh yes, I took the gold,
But, oh, what a price I paid!

'Oh yes, I took the pills.
I followed their advice.
I trusted them all,' she said,
'And now I'm paying the price.

'Oh yes, I was taken in,
Lured by the flicker of fame.
I did not know the cost
Of the way they played the game.

'Oh yes, I'm full of regret,'
She said in a bitter voice.
'I can't have any children.
Thanks to them, I have no choice.

'Oh yes, I took the prize.
I had my glory days.
I was the champion,
But, oh, what a price I've paid.'

## News Flash

Earlier this evening
the penalty shoot-out
between England and Germany
in our back garden
ended in a three–all draw
and the European Cup was shared,
when Alan Shearer
— my brother Billy —
blasted the ball
between the pullovers
we were using for goalposts
with such power
that it flew over the fence
and burst the netting
which Mr Thomas
was using to protect his raspberries,
and Mr Thomas was so angry
that he drove his fork
through the ball
and punctured it.

## Show Me Your Scar, Please, Grandad

'Show me your scar, please, Grandad.
Show me the scar on your knee.
Tell me the story, please, Grandad,
Of how you fell out of the tree.'

Grandad rolled up his trousers
To show me the wrinkled skin
And pointed out where the doctor
Had put all the stitches in.

'We were having a game of football
One afternoon after tea,
When your Great-Uncle Bill miskicked
And the ball got stuck up the tree.

'We tried throwing sticks to knock it out
But we didn't have any luck.
Most of them missed and the others bounced off
'Cause the ball was firmly stuck.

'So we fetched the ladder from the shed
And propped it against the tree,
And I climbed to the top and caught hold
Of a branch to try to shake the ball free.

'I leaned over too far and my foot slipped.
The branch broke with a crack.
I fell through the tree and the next thing I knew
I was lying on the ground on my back.

'I looked down at my leg. There was blood everywhere
And a terrible pain in my knee.
Bill took one look, then ran off to fetch help,
Shouting, "Jack's fallen out of the tree!"

'An ambulance came and they took me away,
Put in stitches and bandaged my knee,
And that's how I came to get this scar
The day I fell out of the tree.'

## How Old Are You, Grandad?

'How old are you Grandad?'
my little sister asked.
Grandad grinned.
'As old as my tongue,' he said,
'And nearly as old as my teeth.'
'What about your hair?' she asked.
Grandad laughed
and stroked his bald head.
'That's a different matter,' he said.

## Borrowed Time

Great-Gran is ninety-six.
'I'm living on borrowed time,'
she said.

'Who did you borrow it from?'
asked my little sister.

'Never you mind,' said Gran.

'I hope you said thank you,'
said my sister.

Great-Gran laughed.
'I do,' she said.
'Every single day.'

## *There's a New Wooden Seat*

There's a new wooden seat
Down by the church gate
Where I sometimes sit
If the bus is late.

And I read the words
On the bright brass plaque:
In Loving Memory
Of Stanley Black.

And I think of the man
With the silvery hair,
Who used to enjoy
The view from there.

And I smile recalling
The pleasure I had
When I stood there
Beside Grandad.

## I Stood All Alone in the Playground

I stood all alone in the playground
At breaktime today.
I didn't feel like playing the games
The others wanted to play.

I stood all alone in the playground,
Trying not to cry,
Thinking of Nan and wondering why
Old people have to die.

## My Little Sister

My little sister used to get on my nerves.

She'd borrow things without asking,
then put them back in the wrong place.

When my friends came round,
she'd pester them
until they'd let her play with them.

If there was something I wanted to watch,
she'd refuse to change channels
unless I bribed her.

When she woke up in the middle of the night,
she'd crawl in beside me
and wake me up with her wriggling.

My little sister used to get on my nerves.
But the bedroom seems so empty without her
And I miss her terribly.

## *How Strange*

How strange to think that someone else
Lived in this house before,
That other people climbed these stairs
And stood on my bedroom floor.

Who was the child who once slept here?
Was it a girl or boy?
What were the dreams that they dreamed?
What was their favourite toy?

How strange to think that someone else
Will live here when I've gone.
Will no one feel my presence here
When I'm the one who's moved on?

## My Baby Brother's Secrets

When my baby brother
wants to tell me a secret,
he comes right up close.
But instead of putting his lips
against my ear,
he presses his ear
tightly against my ear.
Then, he whispers so softly
that I can't hear
a word he's saying.

My baby brother's secrets
are safe with me.


## Moods

Some days
A dark cloud
Fills my mind.
Everything's dull
As if someone
Has drawn a blind
Blotting out the sunlight.

Other days
A stream of light
Fills my mind.
Everything's bright
As if someone
Has thrown open the shutters
Letting the sunlight pour in.

## In My Dream

In my dream,
My older brother is racing along a sandy beach,
Whooping and laughing.

I am trying to keep up with him,
But he is drawing further and further away.

I call for him to wait,
But the wind whisks away my words.

When I tell my mother,
She hugs me.

'Don't worry,' she says.
'All in good time, your turn will come.'

## Museum Pieces

### Exhibit A: Time

This creature is elusive.
It slips by you
In the blink of an eye.
Its tracks stretch endlessly
Backwards into the past,
And eternally
Forwards into the future.
Scientists measure it
In light years,
Athletes in fractions of seconds.
Watch out!
There it goes!

### Exhibit B: Enthusiasm

A vivacious creature,
bright-eyed and bushy-tailed,
found cheering wildly in crowds
or chattering earnestly in small groups.

This specimen was captured
at a model railways exhibition.

May attempt to engage you
in lengthy conversations.

Visitors are, therefore, advised not to linger,
unless they have plenty of time to spare.

This is Rumour — the mischief-maker.
An excitable creature,
His twitching ears always on the alert,
Eavesdropping your every conversation;
His beady eyes scanning the newsprint
For nuggets of scandal;
His forked tongue tasting the air
For tittle-tattle.
He gorges on gossip,
Regurgitating it incessantly.

Visitors are advised
Not to talk in his presence.
Beware — his bark is biting.

## The Space Race

The space race! The space race!
What has it all been for?
Stockpiling satellites
To wage a nuclear war?

The space race! The space race!
Wouldn't it have been more worth
Spending all that money
To improve life here on Earth?

## Space Thought

Locked in my craft I wonder why
Man has this ceaseless urge to try
To solve the mysteries of space,
When Planet Earth itself's a place
Where problems stare you in the face:
The squabblings of the human race.

## I Saw It on the News, Daddy

'I saw it on the news, Daddy.
There was a man with a gun.
Why did he shoot the little girl?
What had she done?'

'She hadn't done anything.
She happened to be in that place,
When the angry man started shooting —
The man from a different race.'

'She was just a little girl, Daddy.
Why did she have to die?
Daddy, I don't understand.'
'Child, neither do I.'

## In a Fit of Rage

In a fit of rage,
He lashed out,
Catching his friend on the jaw.

Tony fell,
Cracking his head
On the stone steps.

He sits in the interview room,
Sobbing out the story,
His head in his hands,
His future shattered.

## All That I Need

'All that I need,'
said the man,
'is a piece of land
on which to grow my crops,
        a school
where my children can be educated,
        a clinic
where my family can receive health care,
        a church
where I can practise my religion,
        a market place
where the prices are fair
and I can speak my mind.'

'All you must do,'
whispered the voice of his father
as he stood by the unmarked grave,
'is keep quiet
and hope to survive.'


## Black Crosses

(On 27 April 1994 black South Africans were able to vote for the
first time in free elections.)

The hands that stole our lands were white.
The hands that forged our cross were white.
This slip of paper is white.
I could crush it in my fist.
My hand trembles
As I make my mark—
A black cross.

## *The African Farmer's Song*

The sun is fierce and hot.
The earth is hard and dry.
Day after day, no rain falls
Out of a cloudless sky.

Oh, bring us some water!
Bring us some rain!
So our fields can all
Grow green again.

The water-hole is empty.
The stream is no longer flowing.
There are no leaves on the trees.
The crops have all stopped growing.

Oh, bring us some water!
Bring us some rain!
So our fields can all
Grow green again.

## Giraffe

Giraffe,
Sometimes
You make me laugh
Way up there
In the skies.

But when
You stoop
To stare at me,
You cut me
Down to size.

## Cats

Fat cat lies
By the living room fire.

Fat cat yawns.
Fat cat stirs.

Fat cat stretches.
Fat cat purrs.

Thin cat slinks
By the garden fence.

Thin cat's eyes
Are narrow slits.

Thin cat hisses.
Thin cat spits.

## The Guard Dog

I'm a gruff dog, a rough dog,
I'm good in a fight.
Keep your distance
Or I might bite.

I'm a mean dog, a keen dog,
I'm quick on my paws.
Stand well back
From my vicious jaws.

I'm a proud dog, a loud dog,
Hear me growl.
One false move
And I'll make you howl.

I'm a hard dog, a guard dog,
A dog to fear.
You have been warned.
Don't come near!

## *Insects*

Insects creep,
Insects crawl,
Insects drive you up the wall.

Insects tickle,
Insects bite,
Insects get you in the night.

Insects nibble,
Insects nip,
Insects suck and insects sip.

Insects breed,
Insects hatch,
Insects make you scratch, scratch, scratch.

Insects here,
Insects there,
Insects in your underwear.

Insects creep,
Insects crawl,
Insects drive me up the wall.

## The Bedbug's Story

'When I was young and handsome,'
The ancient bedbug said,
'I lived in a royal palace
And slept in a royal bed.

'They called me the most fearless
Bug that has ever been.
I'm the bug that bit the bottoms
Of the king and of the queen!'

# Bird Talk

## Percy the Parrot
I'm Percy the Parrot.
If you didn't want me to comment,
Why did you teach me to talk?
I can swear like a trooper
Or bid you 'Good morning'
As politely as any butler.
The choice is yours.
The choice is yours.
The choice is yours.

## Smith the Sparrow
I'm Smith the Sparrow.
Common or garden, that's me.
The bird in the street.
I know my place.
The window-ledge or the gutter,
It's all the same to me.
I'm no high-flier,
Just one of the many,
Picking up the crumbs,
Taking life as it comes.

## Mr Vulture
I'm Mr Vulture,
Happy to be of service,
When there's a carcass needs disposing.
Why am I still circling?
Just biding my time.
I didn't mean to offend you
When I said,
'I've a bone to pick with you.'

## There's a Spring in Your Step

There's a spring in your step
   as you march into April
and the daffodils nod in the breeze.
There's a spring in your step
   as you march into April
and the blossom brightens the trees.

There's a spring in your step
   as you march into April
and the lambs gambol on the grass.
There's a spring in your step
   as you march into April
and winter fades away as you pass.

There's a spring in your step
   as you march into April
and the sun climbs higher in the sky.
There's a spring in your step
   as you march into April
and you wave dreary winter goodbye.

## Spring Snow

Snowflakes
Slip from the sky
Like soft white butterflies,
Brush the trees with their flimsy wings,
Vanish.

## Spring Sunshine

Between showers,
Slices of sunshine
Slant through the windows:
Shafts of primrose
Promising summer.

## Summer

Summer wakes early.
The sun is her alarm clock.
She is washed and dressed
And out in the garden long before breakfast.
She bustles about all morning
Fussing over her flowers.
At noon, she straightens her back,
Acknowledges the sun with a wave,
Then bends once more
To spend the long afternoon and early evening
Tending her precious plants.
At twilight, she casts a quick glance
To assure herself
All's well with her charges,
Then hurries off
To snatch a few hours' sleep
Before the sun rouses her again.

## Gathering Storm

The bright sunlight disappeared
Behind an angry cloud.
The birdsong faltered.
Caught in gusts of wind
Leaves shivered, branches groaned.
The scudding sky loured.
I shuddered
As the day changed its face.

## What Is Fog?

Puffs of dragon smoke
Curling round hedges and trees.

Clouds of steam from a giant's kettle
Pouring out over the city.

The breath from a dinosaur's nostrils
Blurring the world into a grey shadow.

## *Heatwave*

All day
the choking heat
made us wilt.

At night
we lay gasping
in the still air
like stranded fish.

Towards dawn
we fell into a fitful slumber,
only to be awoken
by the sun's fierce rays
heralding another scorcher.

## *Cold Snap*

All day
the searing cold
numbed our bones.

At night
we lay huddled
under thick blankets,
cocooned against the cold.

Towards dawn
we awoke
and crept shivering
from our burrow
to brave another bitter day.

## Last Night It Froze

There are ferns of frost on the window pane
And ice on the puddles in the lane.

Tufts of grass stick up like spikes.
It's far too slippery to ride our bikes.

Icicles hang like spears from the gutters.
The car engine whines and coughs and splutters.

The leaves on the trees are stiff and white.
While we slept, it froze last night.

## It's Diwali Tonight!

Everything's ready to greet the new year.
Everything's bright with light.
Everyone's dressed up and full of joy.
It's Diwali tonight!

We've lit the lamps to show the way
Up to our front door.
We've sprinkled coloured powders to make
Pictures on the floor.

We've given each other gifts of sweets.
There's lots of delicious things to eat.

Everything's ready to greet the new year.
Everything's bright with light.
Everyone's dressed up and full of joy.
It's Diwali tonight!


## On New Year's Eve

Wise as an owl the old year blinks
And silent into shadows sinks.

A secret bud the new year waits
And beckons from beyond the gates.

His memories packed, the traveller stands
And steps in hope across the sands.

## I Spun a Star

(A rondelet)

I spun a star
Which gleamed and glittered in the night.
I spun a star,
Stood watching spellbound from afar,
Until it disappeared from sight,
A shimmering speck of silver light.
I spun a star.

## December Day

December Day
        the ground
        brittle with frost
        crunches
        beneath your feet.
Trees
        shorn of their leaves
        shiver
        in the thin wind
        thrusting their branches
        defiantly
        skywards

        while their roots dig deeper

        seeking succour in the soil.